BOBSLEDDING AND THE LUGE

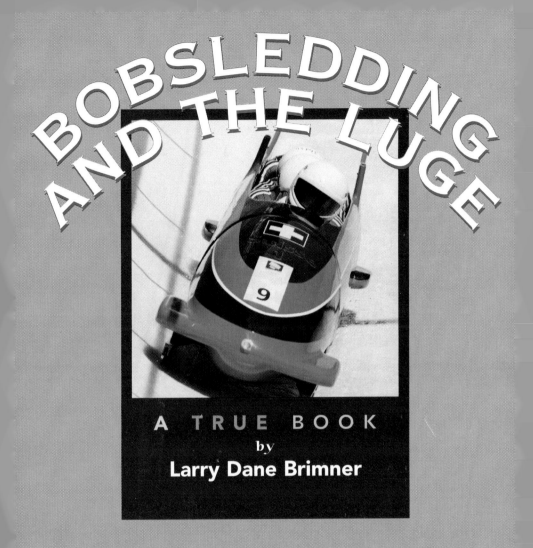

A TRUE BOOK

by
Larry Dane Brimner

Children's Press®
A Division of Grolier Publishing
New York London Hong Kong Sydney
Danbury, Connecticut

Reading Consultant
Linda Cornwell
Learning Resource Consultant
Indiana Department
of Education

Author's Dedication
For Sneed B. Collard III

A bobsled team pushes their sled at the beginning of the race.

Library of Congress Cataloging-in-Publication Data

Brimner, Larry Dane.
    Bobsledding and the luge / by Larry Dane Brimner.
       p.   cm. — (A true book)
    Includes bibliographical references (p.) and index.
    Summary: Describes the history of bobsledding and luge competi-
tion, with a look at these sports at the Olympics.
    ISBN 0-516-20436-X (lib. bdg.)   0-516-26203-3 (pbk.)
    1. Bobsledding—Juvenile literature. [1. Bobsledding. 2. Olympics.]
I. Title. II. Series.
GV856.B75 1997   97-2271
796.9'5—dc21   CIP
                                                         AC

Contents

A bobsled speeds through a turn.

Down the Chute!

A bobsled rockets down the icy chute. The driver and crew are tucked low to help increase their speed. They lean, preparing to round a curve. As they do, the bobsled climbs the frozen walls of the chute. For a moment, it seems as if the bobsled might leave the chute completely and launch into space. It doesn't! Instead, the bobsled explodes out of the curve. It speeds down the chute toward the finish line. Will the crew win the race?

Bobsled racing began in the winter of 1888–89 when an Englishman had an idea. He was in Switzerland and noticed that sleds were used to haul wood over the snow and ice.

In the past, sleds were necessary to gather wood during the winter.

Wood-hauling sleds were practical tools in snowy Switzerland. They were also simple in design. Two wooden runners slid over the frozen surface. Wood for winter fires was piled on animal skins that stretched between the runners. The Englishman wondered if a sled could also be used for racing.

He tied two of the sleds together. For a brake, he attached a rake that he could drag in the snow. Then he took off down a slope. It was a success! And the activity quickly caught on with wealthy people.

They formed racing clubs and held contests. The original races were held on icy roads

One of the first
bobsled runs

and mountain passes, but people wanted greater speed. To achieve this, racers would lean back and jerk forward. This "bobbing" motion gave the sport its name.

Still, racers wanted to go even faster, so they built special raceways, called "bobruns." They were coated with ice and had steep sides. The steep sides kept the bobsled on the run, which allowed it to go faster. In the winter of 1889–90,

the first steel sled was intro-
duced. It went faster still.
Since then, people have continued to work on new
designs, which use stronger,
lightweight materials to
increase the sled's speed.

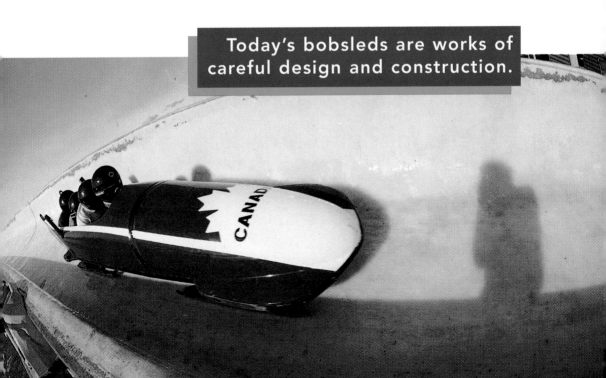

Today's bobsleds are works of careful design and construction.

Bobsledding Today

Bobsledding has been part of the Olympics since the first Winter Games in 1924. The only time the event did not take place was in 1960, when weather and time kept a bob-sled run from being built. Today's bobsleds, however, do not look like those used at the first Olympic Winter Games.

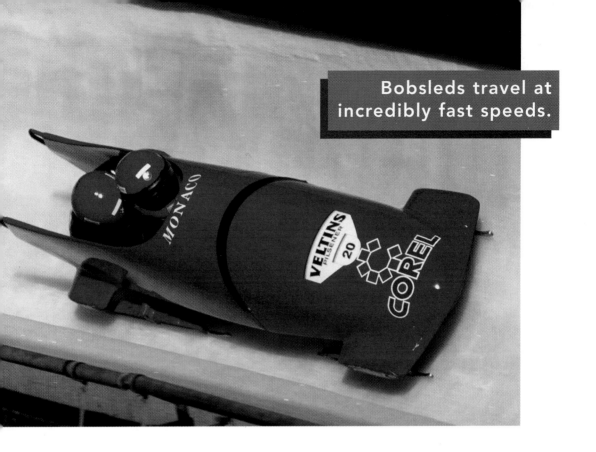

Bobsleds travel at incredibly fast speeds.

Today's sleds are built of fiberglass and steel. Looking more like missiles than wood-hauling sleds, they skim over ice at lightning-fast speeds. Without goggles, it would be impossible for racers to see.

13

A two-man bobsled (top) and a
four-man bobsled (bottom)

Bobsleds come in two sizes,
one for two-man teams and the
other for four-man teams.
(Women do not yet compete at
the Olympic level in bobsledding.) A two-man sled cannot
weigh more than 390 kilograms
(859 pounds), including the riders.

A four-man sled is limited to 630 kilograms (1,389 pounds). Weight and gravity carry the sled and riders down the bobrun.

Bobruns have also changed. Today's courses twist and turn. They are concrete chutes that are refrigerated for the best possible ice conditions.

Beneath the bobrun ice is a base of concrete.

One of the most important parts of a race is the start. Racers run and push the sled into the chute. To keep from slipping, they wear cleated shoes that grip the ice. They must work as a team to push the sled as fast as possible. Their timing must be perfect.

Gaining speed, they leap into the bobsled right at the starting line. The man in front steers. The man at the rear operates the brake. Only the

At a precise moment, the bobsled crew jumps into the sled (top). The driver's head stays up while the other crew members crouch low (bottom).

driver keeps his head up. The others tuck themselves low so they will go as fast as they possibly can. (Racers no longer bob their upper bodies.)

The bobsled explodes down the run, hitting speeds of 100 miles (161 kilometers) per hour and greater. One error could spell disaster. At this speed, a crash could result in injury—or death. From start to finish, a record-breaking race lasts less than a minute. And each run is a dangerous new adventure.

This bobsled crashed and turned over after taking a turn too quickly.

Olympic Sportsmanship

A shining example of the Olympic Creed was the Italian bobsledder Eugenio Monti. He was known to be a fierce competitor. But he was also a fair-minded sportsman.

Monti had fought unsuccessfully for twelve years to win a gold medal in the two-man bobsled event. At the 1964 Games in Innsbruck, Austria, he was once again in the running for a gold medal.

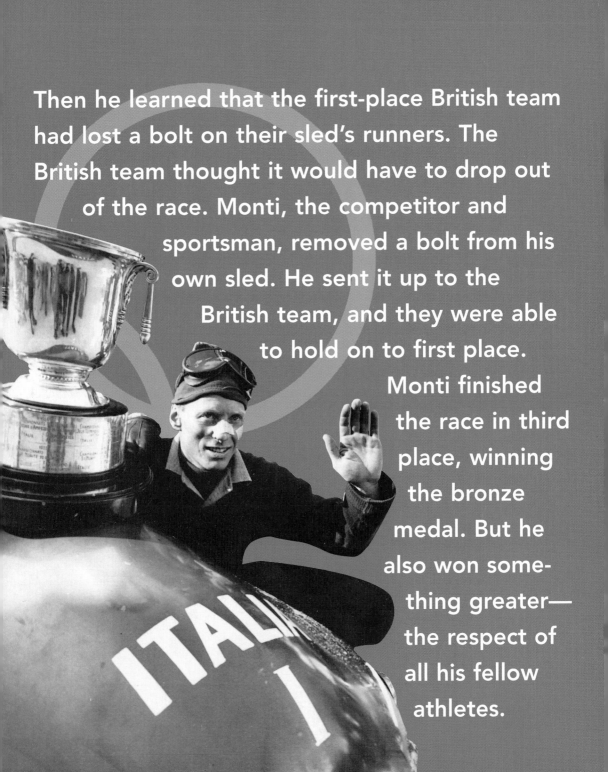

Then he learned that the first-place British team had lost a bolt on their sled's runners. The British team thought it would have to drop out of the race. Monti, the competitor and sportsman, removed a bolt from his own sled. He sent it up to the British team, and they were able to hold on to first place. Monti finished the race in third place, winning the bronze medal. But he also won something greater— the respect of all his fellow athletes.

The Luge

Like bobsledders, luge racers shoot down steep, ice-covered tracks. Both men and women compete in this sport, though in separate events. Men compete against each other in one- and two-person events. Women compete only in one-person events.

Luge takes place on a track
similar to a bobsled run.

A two-person
luge team

Luge sleds are similar to toboggans, and the racers are called "sliders."

Luge is one of the most dangerous sports in the Olympics. Lying on their backs, sliders rocket down runs feet first. They steer their sleds with gentle leg and shoulder pressure. To increase their speed, sliders wear suits, helmets, and special pointed booties. A practiced slider reaches speeds up to

80 miles (128 kilometers) per hour.

To start a race, sliders rock back and forth on their sleds. Then they push off with force. They wear spiked gloves and use their hands to catch the ice and thrust themselves forward. This helps to increase their speed. Then gravity takes over, and it's a downhill race against the clock to the end of the run.

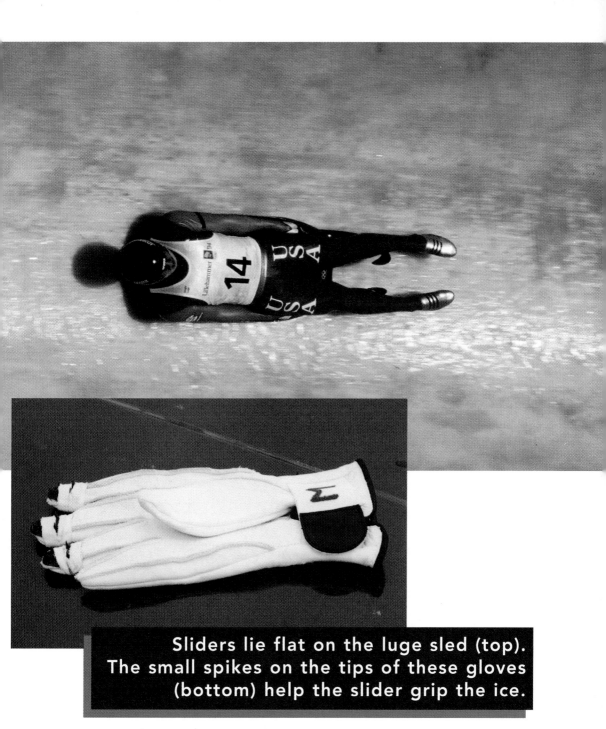

Sliders lie flat on the luge sled (top).
The small spikes on the tips of these gloves
(bottom) help the slider grip the ice.

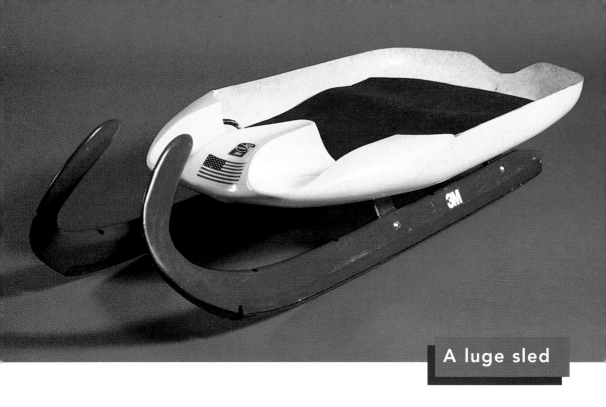

A luge sled

Luge sleds are speed machines. Wood, fiberglass, or plastic runners support hardened steel blades. To make the sled even faster, sliders polish and sharpen the blades again and again.

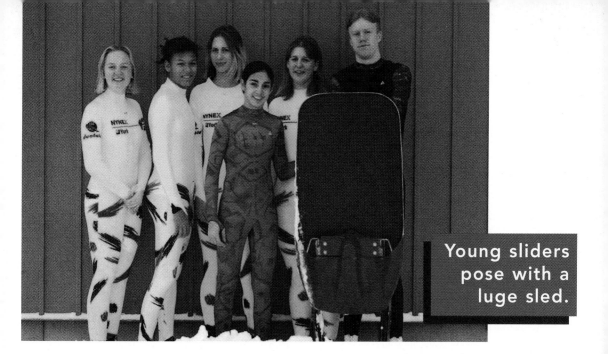

Although luge competition dates back to 1883, it has been part of the Winter Olympic Games only since 1964. All seventy-two Olympic luge medals have been won by four countries—Germany, Austria, Italy, and the U.S.S.R. (Russia).

What a Run!

Bobsled and luge runs are extremely difficult to build and maintain. There are only a small number of them in the world today. Each one offers different kinds of excitement and challenges to sliders. Some are short and full of twists. Others are straight and steep. Here are four different luge runs from around the world:

Start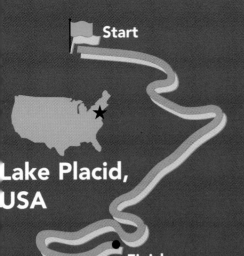

Lake Placid, USA

Finish

	Length	Curves
Men	930m	14
Women	740m	11

Nagano, Japan

Start

Finish

	Length	Curves
Men	1326m	14
Women	1194m	13

Start

Königsee, Germany

Finish

	Length	Curves
Men	1300m	16
Women	1225m	12

Start

Calgary, Canada

Finish

	Length	Curves
Men	1251m	14
Women	1185m	10

A New Twist

People are always inventing new ways to play old sports. A new twist to luge is street luge. Street luge has been around since the early 1980s. It's a blend of ice luge and skateboarding.

Street luge uses a stretched-out skateboard that is usually

Street luge takes place on road surfaces, not ice.

built of a light metal called
aluminum. A slider, or pilot,
rides it the same way one
rides an ice luge—with no

Several sets of wheels allow the sled to move down a run.

seat belt or brakes. Instead of rocketing down an icy chute, however, a street luge pilot zooms along just inches above asphalt.

Like luge, street luge is a high-speed, high-risk sport. Pilots must wear special gear to protect themselves against injury. A leather suit is specially fitted to each slider. Ultra-padded gloves are needed. Many street lugers also wear motorcycle helmets.

Street luge is not yet part of the Olympics. Still, street luge racers do compete against each other. The International Luge Road Racing Association

Street luge is featured at the Extreme Games.

organizes many events. Also, street luge and other unusual, high-speed sports are featured every year at the Extreme Games. They are called the "Extreme Games" because of the dangerous nature of the sports.

Olympic Moments

The Olympic Winter Games have always been a celebration of the athletes of winter. Naturally, sliders wanted to be a part of it. When they asked that their sport be made a part of the Winter Games, however, critics argued that luge was too

It is always a scary moment when a slider loses control of the sled.

dangerous. In 1964, sliders were finally given a chance. Unfortunately, luge in the Olympics got off to a sad beginning. Two weeks before the 1964 Games were to open, there was a serious accident. Kazimierz Kay-Skrzypeski, a Polish-born British slider, was killed on a trial run of the Olympic course.

The Olympics are a stage for triumph as well as tragedy. In 1928, Billy Fiske was chosen to drive the four-man bobsled for the United States. He was only sixteen years old. By leading the team to victory, he became the youngest man

ever to win a gold medal at the Winter Olympics. That record has since been broken by Scott Allen, a fourteen-year-old figure skater. Still, Billy's victory was a big achievement for one so young.

Bobsledding and the luge are two of the fastest sports at the Olympics. Participants are like human missiles on a

The winning U.S. bobsled team poses in their sled with other runner-up teams.

Bobsledding (top) and luge (bottom) are two of the fastest sports in the Winter Olympics.

wild roller-coaster ride. In each sport, the goal is to flash to the bottom of the run in record time. Yet the racers are never happy at the bottom of a run. There is always a new record to break, a new run to conquer, and a new competitor to challenge. So they return to the top again and again for another wild ride down the chute.

To Find Out More

Here are some additional resources to help you learn more about bobsledding and the luge:

 **Books**

Duden, Jane. **The Olympics.** Macmillan Child Group, 1991.

Greenspan, Bud. **100 Greatest Moments in Olympic History.** General Publishing Group, 1995.

Harris, Jack C. **The Winter Olympics.** Creative Education, Inc., 1990.

Malley, Stephen. **A Kid's Guide to the Nineteen Ninety-Four Winter Olympics.** Bantam Press, 1994.

Wallechinsky, David. **The Complete Book of the Winter Olympics.** Little, Brown & Co., 1993.

 **Organizations**

U.S. Bobsled and Skeleton Federation (UBSF)
Box 828
Lake Placid, NY 12946

United States Luge Association (USLA)
PO Box 651
35 Church Street
Lake Placid, NY 12946

Internet Sites

2002 Winter Olympic Games Home Page
www.SLC2002.org

A growing web page that provides information on the 2002 Winter Olympics in Salt Lake City.

International Federation of Bobsledding and Tobogganing
www.fibt.corel.com

A list of events and new developments in bobsledding from around the world.

Official 1998 Olympic Web Site
www.nagano.olympic.org

A great source of information on the events of the 1998 Winter Olympics.

Original Luge Home Page
www.luge.com

Learn about the different equipment and techniques necessary to ride the luge.

Skateluge Home Page
www.skateluge.com

Information about skateluge equipment and how to start sliding.

Winter Sports Page
http://www.wintersports.org

A central site to explore winter sports and links to other sites.

Important Words

aluminum light metal used in the construction of bobsleds and luges

blade the part of the bobsled that runs on the ice

bobrun a course designed for a bobsled race

bootie race shoes specially designed for sliders

chute a track with high sides that is specially designed and built for a bobsled

fiberglass a light and strong material used to build bobsleds and luges

runner the part of the bobsled that holds the blades

slider someone who rides on the luge

46

Index

Meet the Author

Larry Dane Brimner is the author of several books for Children's Press, including five True Books on the Winter Olympics. He is a member of the Authors Guild and the Society of Children's Book Writers and Illustrators. Mr. Brimner makes his home in Southern California and the Rocky Mountains.

C
L
E
V
E
L
A
N
D

RICHARD RAMBECK

THE HISTORY OF THE

INDIANS

CREATIVE EDUCATION

Published by Creative Education
123 South Broad Street, Mankato, Minnesota 56001
Creative Education is an imprint of The Creative Company

Designed by Rita Marshall
Editorial assistance by Julie Bach and John Nichols

Photos by: Allsport Photography, AP/Wide World, Archive Photos,
SportsChrome.

Library of Congress Cataloging-in-Publication Data

Rambeck, Richard.
The History of the Cleveland Indians / by Richard Rambeck.
p. cm. — (Baseball)
Summary: Highlights the key personalities and memorable games in the
history of the team that has played in the American League as the Indians
since 1916.
ISBN: 0-88682-906-2

1. Cleveland Indians (Baseball team)—History—Juvenile literature.
[1. Cleveland Indians (Baseball team)—History. 2. Baseball—History.]
I. Title. II. Series: Baseball (Mankato, Minn.)

GV875.C7R355   1999
796.357'64'0977132—dc21   97-7133

First edition

9 8 7 6 5 4 3 2 1

Cleveland, Ohio, sits on the shores of Lake Erie, one of the five Great Lakes of North America. With nearly two million people, the Cleveland metropolitan area is an economic center and a busy port. Ships carrying goods along the St. Lawrence Seaway dock at Cleveland's waterfront.

Dominating the view from just about any location in the city, Lake Erie is responsible for many of Cleveland's weather patterns, as heavy winds often blow inland off the lake. One of the structures most affected by the Lake Erie winds is Jacobs Field, home of the American League's Cleveland Indians. Both the stadium and the team are a source of

Cy Young played in Cleveland from 1909 to 1911.

pride for the people of northeastern Ohio, who know that the history of baseball in Cleveland goes back a long way.

In 1869, Cleveland, known then as the "Forest City," hosted a team called—appropriately enough—the "Forest Citys." In 1889 the team's name was changed to the "Spiders," partly because many of the players were tall and thin. The team then rapidly went through three names—the "Blues," the "Broncos," and the "Naps"—before settling on the Indians in 1915.

The people of Cleveland chose this name in honor of Louis M. Sockalexis, a Penobscot Indian from Old Town, Maine, who was the first Native American to play major league baseball. Sockalexis joined the Cleveland team in 1897. He played for only three seasons, but compiled a batting average of .333. When the club was looking for a new name in 1914, a fan submitted "Indians" to a local newspaper contest, explaining that it would be a testament to the game's first Native American Indian.

1 9 1 0

The legendary "Shoeless" Joe Jackson joined the Indians in 1910 and batted .408 the following season.

SPEAKER AND "SARGE": FIRST INDIANS STARS

Before 1916, Cleveland fans had little to cheer about, but that started to change, partly because of the talents of star center fielder Tris Speaker. With Speaker's fielding and hitting, the Indians began moving up in the American League standings. Speaker became the Indians' manager in 1919, and he and pitcher Jim "Sarge" Bagby gave the Cleveland fans hope for an American League pennant. But first the team would have to cope with a terrible tragedy.

Home run threat David Justice.

1 9 3 3

Hal Trosky drove in 142 runs to win the AL Rookie of the Year award.

On August 20, 1920, the Indians were in New York for a first-place showdown with the Yankees. Cleveland shortstop Ray Chapman, who was Speaker's best friend, was hit on the head by a pitch from New York's Carl Mays. The blow fractured Chapman's skull, and 12 hours later he died in a New York hospital. He was the only player ever killed as a result of an injury suffered in a major-league game. The grief-stricken Speaker and the rest of the Indians didn't want to continue playing, but they soon decided to dedicate the season—and their pennant hopes—to Chapman's memory.

Cleveland went on to win its first American League pennant, earning the right to play the Brooklyn Dodgers in a best-of-nine World Series. Led by Bagby, who won the crucial fifth game with the series tied two games apiece, the Indians won the championship five games to two. It was a great moment in Cleveland sports history.

CLEVELAND FINDS FELLER ON THE FARM

Cleveland and the rest of the American League took a back seat to the powerful New York Yankees throughout the 1920s and then the Philadelphia Athletics and the Detroit Tigers in the 1930s. Then, in 1936, they found a player who would eventually pitch them back to the top.

"Gentlemen," said Cleveland scout Cy Slapnicka at a private luncheon, "I've found the greatest young pitcher I ever saw. I suppose this sounds like the same old stuff to you, but I want you to believe me. This boy that I found out in Iowa will be the greatest pitcher the world has ever known. I only saw him pitch once before I signed him." The other team executives looked excitedly at Slapnicka. Who was this guy, they wanted to know. "Bob Feller," Slapnicka told them. "When can we see him?" they asked. "Bob's finishing out his school term," Slapnicka said, "but I repeat to you, gentlemen, he will be the star of them all. Do you know that he averaged 19 strikeouts a game last summer?"

The executives were impressed, but many of them thought Feller was finishing out his college term. When Slapnicka told them Feller was a 17-year-old high school student, many wondered if the scout hadn't lost his mind. A week later, they all found out about Feller, the polite farm boy with a devastating fastball. He pitched three innings for the Indians in an exhibition game against the St. Louis Cardinals. Steve O'Neill, the Cleveland catcher who doubled as manager, caught two of the innings and then came to the bench complaining of a sore hand. "That kid's too tough for me to catch," O'Neill said. "He throws that thing so fast it looks like a pea."

The Cardinals must have felt the same way, as Feller struck out eight of the nine St. Louis batters he faced. After the game, a photographer asked Cardinals pitcher Dizzy Dean, a future Hall-of-Famer, if he'd pose with Feller. "Why ask me?" Dean laughed. "Ask the kid if he'll pose with me!"

A few weeks later, Feller struck out 15 St. Louis Browns batters in his first regular-season game. In his next game, he matched Dizzy Dean's major-league strikeout record by fanning 17 Philadelphia Athletics. Feller soon became the talk of the American League. By the time he was in his early 20s, Feller was consistently winning at least 20 games a season. When the U.S. became involved in World War II in 1941, and young men were called to fight for their country,

1 9 4 0

Bob Feller became the first pitcher in history to throw a no-hitter on Opening Day.

The hard-hitting Julio Franco.

Cory Snyder, a quick outfielder.

1 9 4 7

Cleveland out-fielder Larry Doby became the American League's first-ever black player.

Feller enlisted in the Navy. He missed four full seasons while in the service, but when he returned to baseball, he was as good as ever, winning 26 games in 1946. With Feller and shortstop Lou Boudreau, who was also the manager, the Indians had hopes of contending for a pennant.

In 1948 the Indians won their first six games and were still in first place on June 30, much to the amazement of the other teams in the league. "Don't worry about the Indians," said one American League manager. "They'll fall apart; they always do." But the Indians didn't fall apart; Boudreau wouldn't let them. The Cleveland shortstop batted .355 and was named the American League Most Valuable Player. The Indians also got outstanding performances from veteran pitchers Bob Lemon and the ageless LeRoy "Satchel" Paige, a former Negro-league star who finally made his major-league debut in his late 40s.

At the end of the season, the Indians and the Boston Red Sox were tied for first place in the American League, forcing a one-game playoff to decide who would win the pennant. Neither Feller nor Lemon was available to pitch the playoff game, but it really didn't matter who was on the mound, because Boudreau destroyed the Red Sox with two home runs and two singles. Cleveland defeated Boston 8–3 to advance to the World Series against another Boston team, the Braves.

In the World Series, Feller's effectiveness was reduced by a sore arm. But Lemon, who had posted a 20–14 record during the regular season, was razor-sharp. Lemon won both of his starts as the Indians defeated the Braves four games to two, giving Cleveland its second World Series title.

The Indians remained one of the top teams in the American League for several seasons, but they weren't able to win another pennant until 1954. That year, Cleveland put together the most victories ever by an American League team in a season, winning 111 and losing only 43. The main reason for the team's success was outstanding pitching. Lemon and Early Wynn each won 23 games. Mike Garcia posted a 19–8 record, and Feller, at the ripe old age of 35, compiled an excellent 13–3 mark.

The Indians were favored to defeat the New York Giants in the World Series, but it was not to be. Willie Mays and the rest of the Giants, displaying incredible hitting and fielding, swept the Indians in four straight games. The 1954 season was the final moment of glory for several Cleveland stars, including Feller, who retired after the 1956 season.

After the previous year's disappointing finish, Al Lopez was named the new manager of the Indians.

"SUDDEN SAM" STRIKES FEAR IN HITTERS

When Bob Feller retired, Cleveland fans wondered if they would ever again see a pitcher who threw as hard as he did. It seemed unlikely that another Feller would come along, but there was nothing likely about Sam McDowell, a left-handed pitcher who was called "the next Bob Feller" when he joined the Indians as an 18-year-old rookie in 1961. While growing up, McDowell never expected he would be good enough to become a major-leaguer. "I never really wanted to be a baseball player like the rest of the kids," McDowell recalled. "But my father saw I had talent, so he forced me into it. But I never thought I was that good at it. Even when I made the majors, I used to start every game with the hope I just wouldn't embarrass myself out there."

McDowell didn't have to worry about that. His fastball became one of the most feared in the major leagues. He soon acquired the nickname "Sudden Sam" because, as one player claimed, McDowell's pitches got to the plate "all of a sudden, man, all of a sudden." Some experts called McDowell the most talented pitcher in the majors. Said Oakland A's pitcher John "Blue Moon" Odom, "If I had Sudden's stuff, I'd win 25 games every year."

But McDowell wasn't interested in winning 25 games every year; he was more concerned with overcoming personal challenges. "The only thing I get satisfaction from is accomplishing something I'm not supposed to be able to do," he stated. "I live for challenges, and once I overcome them, I have to go on to something new." McDowell's biggest challenge in life proved to be overcoming alcoholism. Although he eventually quit drinking after his playing days, the hard-throwing pitcher's career was lessened by his hard living style. "Baseball was easy for me," observed McDowell in retirement. "But life was hard."

In most cases, McDowell made life hard on American League hitters too, but Oakland A's slugger Reggie Jackson enjoyed facing Sudden Sam. "You know he's going to challenge you, his strength against yours, and either you beat him, or he beats you," Jackson said.

In spite of McDowell's talent, the Indians didn't enjoy much success during the 1960s. McDowell was named to the American League All-Star team six times, but he never came close to leading his team to a pennant. Cleveland had few

1 9 6 2

Veteran right-hander Dick Donovan paced Cleveland starters with 20 wins and a 3.59 ERA.

Knuckleball specialist Tom Candiotti.

Slugging outfielder Rocky Colavito.

stars besides McDowell and power-hitting outfielder Rocky Colavito, who led the American League in homers (42) in 1959 and runs batted in (108) in 1965. The Indians' roster was bolstered in 1971 by the addition of first baseman Chris Chambliss, who hit .275, drove in 48 runs, and was named Rookie of the Year in the American League.

McDowell's last year in Cleveland was 1971. He was traded in the off-season to the San Francisco Giants for veteran pitcher Gaylord Perry. When McDowell left Cleveland, he was second on the Indians' all-time strikeout list with 2,281. McDowell's total put him only 300 strikeouts behind the legendary Bob Feller, though Feller had pitched seven more seasons for the Indians than McDowell had. Oddly, after leaving the Indians, McDowell never regained the form that had made him one of the top pitchers in baseball. Gaylord Perry, however, came to Cleveland in top form, and he would baffle hitters even more than McDowell had.

1 9 6 5

Sam McDowell established a team record for left-handers by striking out 325 batters.

PERRY'S PITCHES PRODUCE SUCCESS

When Gaylord Perry joined the Indians, he made it clear that he wouldn't settle for second best. Perry stated his philosophy: "You should do everything possible to win—short of scratching the other guy's eyes out." Opponents believed Perry cheated to win by using illegal substances on the ball to make it dip and dive. They accused him of putting everything from Vaseline to hair cream on the ball to get an edge. Even some of his teammates claimed Perry threw spitballs.

"Gaylord goes through all those goofy motions before he

A powerhouse '80s slugger, Joe Carter (pages 18-19).

Pitcher Gaylord Perry's 24 wins and 1.92 ERA earned him a spot on the AL All-Star Team roster.

pitches," laughed Indians outfielder Oscar Gamble. "He touches the bill of his hat, then the back of his hat, then he'll dig around in his glove; guys are so busy trying to figure out where he's hiding the stuff that they forget to try and hit him."

Perry said he never threw a spitball, but rather a forkball, a pitch that drops suddenly as it nears the plate. When Perry threw one of his forkballs, which dropped a great deal, the opposing team would claim it was a spitball and ask the umpire to search Perry for grease or some other substance.

Sometimes Perry practically had to undress on the mound so the umpire could search him, which angered his manager, Ken Aspromonte. "It's just that Gaylord is always the goat," the Cleveland manager said. "He has the reputation, so they [umpires] pick on him. Why don't they spread these searches around? Why just my guy?" During his years in Cleveland, Perry was searched countless times, but umpires never found any evidence on the wily veteran.

Perry's pitches, spitters or not, were almost unhittable in 1972. He won an amazing 24 games for a team that was never in contention for the pennant. For his efforts, Perry was selected as the American League Cy Young Award winner; he is the only Cleveland pitcher ever to receive that honor, which was first given in 1956. But the Cleveland club, even with Perry's heroics, remained near the bottom of the seven-team American League East Division throughout the 1970s and into the 1980s.

In an effort to reverse this trend, Perry was traded after a few successful seasons. Cleveland fans then had to root for such other stars as outfielder Joe Charboneau, who won the 1980 Rookie of the Year honor in the American League after batting .289, slugging 23 homers, and driving in 87 runs. But Charboneau's star fell as quickly as it rose; he went into a long slump during the 1981 season and was sent down to the minor leagues. First baseman Andre Thornton picked up the slack by hitting 32 homers in 1982 and 33 more in 1984. In 1985, despite the presence of such power hitters as Thornton, Joe Carter, and Mel Hall, the Indians lost 102 games, tying the record for the most losses in franchise history. Cleveland rallied to post a winning season in 1986, and fans started to flock to the old Municipal Stadium to see Carter, right fielder Cory Snyder, and pitchers Tom Candiotti and Greg Swindell. The Indians, however, were unable to build on this success and failed to become a championship-caliber team.

After a disappointing 1989 season, in which the team fin-

1 9 8 2

Andre Thornton tallied 116 RBIs, the highest total in almost three decades of Cleveland baseball.

Spitball pitcher or not, Gaylord Perry was a winner.

Former Indians closer Doug Jones.

ished sixth in the AL East with a 73–89 record, club officials decided to make a bold move. Joe Carter, one of the most feared sluggers in the American League, was traded to San Diego in a multiplayer deal that included young catcher Sandy Alomar Jr. and second baseman Carlos Baerga.

ALOMAR PROVES TO BE A BIG CATCH

The Indians were sorry to lose Carter, but team officials were easily consoled after seeing Alomar's talents. "I've been in baseball for 29 years," said Cleveland bullpen coach Luis Isaac, "and Sandy Alomar is the best catching prospect I've seen since Johnny Bench." Alomar, who was born in Puerto Rico, certainly was one of the biggest catching prospects—he stands 6-foot-5 and weighs 220 pounds. "You wait and see how much he develops as a hitter," Isaac said before the 1990 season. "He's only 23 years old now. He still has some baby fat. Most Latin players don't mature until they're 26 or 27."

Many Cleveland fans were worried that Alomar wouldn't want to leave San Diego, where his father, Sandy Alomar Sr., was a coach. The catcher's brother, Roberto, was also with the Padres. "I had two feelings when the trade was made," said Sandy, who had been unable to beat out San Diego's All-Star catcher Benito Santiago for the starting position. "The first was that I was happy because I finally would have my chance. The second was that it was sad that the family was being broken up." But if Alomar was homesick during his first season with the Indians, he showed no signs of it. His average hovered near .300 for much of the year while the surprising Cleveland

1 9 8 4

Second baseman Julio Franco set an Indians all-time record with 658 at-bats during the season.

Doc Edwards led the Indians to within 11 games of the division title—their closest finish since 1959.

club fought its way into the middle of the AL East race. Alomar was so impressive that he was voted by the fans to start at catcher for the American League All-Stars, making him the first rookie catcher to ever start an All-Star Game. Although neither Alomar nor the Indians were able to sustain their torrid pace throughout the second half of the season, many signs indicated a promising future.

Infielder Brook Jacoby and outfielders Candy Maldonado, Cory Snyder, and Chris James keyed the Cleveland offense. Starting pitchers Tom Candiotti and Bud Black both had excellent years, and Doug Jones continued to show he was one of the top relief pitchers in the American League.

TRAGEDY HITS A RISING TEAM

Bringing Alomar to the Indians was part of a player development strategy outlined by new owners Richard and David Jacobs, two brothers who bought the Cleveland Indians in 1987. Over the next several years, with players like Alomar and pitchers Steve Olin and Tim Crews, as well as an emphasis on the Indians' farm teams, the Jacobs brothers slowly moved the club into contention.

Success didn't come immediately, but by the spring of 1993, the Indians were ready. Suddenly, at the end of training camp, tragedy struck: Olin and Crews were killed in a boating accident, and a third player, Bob Ojeda, was seriously injured. The other players were grief-stricken; it was the second time in club history that the Indians had to cope with death in their ballclub. Manager Mike Hargrove kept the players on track as best he could, and the team rallied for a successful second half of the season—but it still finished in sixth place in the American League East.

The following year, the Indians' young talent began to blossom. Albert Belle, Kenny Lofton, Carlos Baerga, Sandy Alomar, Charles Nagy, and Jim Thome were no longer prospects—they were now the heart of a pennant contender. It was also the first year of play in Jacobs Field, a new state-of-the-art ballpark that attracted fans from far and wide. But the team's hopes for a pennant were dashed again, this time by a players' strike that brought a halt to the season with the Indians one game out of first place.

When the strike ended in early 1995, the team picked up where it had left off, determined to make 1995 a banner season. The Indians' work and drive paid off when they won the American League Central division by a record 30 games. In the American League Championship Series, Cleveland won a dramatic six-game series over the Seattle Mariners to capture the Indians' first American League pennant in 41 years. "What a moment; what a day for our fans," said ecstatic Indians manager, and former player, Mike Hargrove. "I played here in the bad years, and now to win the pennant. Wow. I'm so thankful to be here to enjoy it with all of our great fans."

The Indians next faced a playoff-hardened Atlanta Braves team in the World Series, and despite standout performances from swift center fielder Kenny Lofton and slugging left fielder Albert Belle, the Indians lost the series four games to two. "I hate to say it, but I think as a young team, we were just happy to be there," said Alomar. "But for us, 1995 was just the beginning."

1 9 9 2

Kenny Lofton swiped 66 bases to lead the American League for the first of five straight seasons.

Hard-hitting first baseman Jim Thome (pages 26-27).

1 9 9 6

Outfielder Albert Belle led the league in runs batted in (148) for the second year in a row.

The talented young Indians were a top class of the American League in 1996. The supremely confident group won 96 games and claimed the AL Central once again. Led by Albert Belle's 48 homers and 148 RBIs and Kenny Lofton's 75 steals and 132 runs scored, the Indians took the league by storm. But something very important was missing.

"Our club in 1996 had great talent, but it lacked chemistry; guys just didn't get along," explained manager Mike Hargrove. "Our clubhouse was always a tense place, and, in the end, I think it affected us on the field." The divided Indians were knocked out in the first round of the American League playoffs by the Baltimore Orioles, three games to one. "We got beat and we deserved it," said pitcher Orel Hershiser. "We all need to examine what happened here." In the offseason, the Indians' front office decided to make major changes. Lofton was dealt to the Atlanta Braves for outfielders Marquis Grissom and David Justice. Slugging third baseman Matt Williams was acquired in a deal with the San Francisco Giants, and outfielder Albert Belle signed with the Chicago White Sox as a free agent.

The Indians' management was gambling that the new players would form an explosive team on the field, while being less explosive off of it. Fortunately for Cleveland fans, the gamble paid off. The Indians battled to a third-straight AL Central title with an 86–75 record.

An instant fan favorite, Justice provided the team with a strong bat and, more importantly, strong leadership. The lanky right fielder boomed 33 homers and drove in 101 runs while batting .329 his first year in Cleveland. "David carried us in a lot of tough spots this year," said first baseman Jim Thome. "He's a guy that knows what it takes to win, whether it's at the plate, in the field, or in the clubhouse."

After being heavy favorites to win it all in 1995 and '96, the Indians began the 1997 postseason in the unfamiliar role of underdog. Without the burden of high expectations to weigh them down, Cleveland surged to a first-round victory over the New York Yankees. Up next for Cleveland would be the mighty Baltimore Orioles with the American League championship at stake. The Indians, riding the hot bats of Justice, Thome, and outfielder Manny Ramirez, along with the gutty pitching of Orel Hershiser, Charles Nagy, and spectacular rookie Jaret Wright, shocked the baseball world by defeating the Orioles four games to two.

In the World Series, the Indians faced the Florida Marlins. The two ballclubs battled fiercely, and after six games the series stood even at three games apiece. In the deciding game seven, the Indians held a 2–1 lead through eight innings on the strength of Wright's stingy pitching. But in the ninth inning, the Marlins rallied to tie the score and force the game into extra innings. The Indians threatened, but it was the Marlins who broke through, scoring the winning run in the bottom of the 11th inning to clinch the series for Florida. "We fought hard, and we made it further than anybody thought we would," Justice said after the series. "It's tough to lose, but I know this team. We'll be back, and next time we'll take the trophy home to Cleveland."

Even with Justice, Alomar, Thome, Ramirez, and Wright on their own, the Indians would be a formidable contender

1 9 9 8

Outfielder Manny Ramirez anticipated his fourth straight season with 25 or more home runs.

The talented Sandy Alomar Jr.

Slick-fielding shortstop Omar Vizquel.

for years to come, but Cleveland's aggressive front office added even more firepower in the 1997 offseason. Superstar Kenny Lofton returned to Cleveland, signing as a free agent, to again spark the Indians' offense from the lead-off spot. All-Star third baseman Travis Fryman was brought over in a trade with the Arizona Diamondbacks to provide power and a sure glove at the hot corner. Veteran pitchers Dwight Gooden and Dave Burba were acquired to beef up the already steady starting rotation.

"This organization is committed to winning championships," said Lofton upon his return. "I wanted to be a part of that when it happens." For the Indians and their fans, the championship stage is set. The former laughingstock franchise of baseball now stands poised to claim the game's greatest prize: a World Series title.